Contents

Comparing the past and present

Things in the past have already happened.

Things in the present are happening now.

Travelling has changed over time.

The way people take trips in the present is very different to the past.

Getting around

In the past most people walked from place to place.

Today, many people only walk
a short way.

In the past many people used horses to travel.

Today, some people ride horses
for fun.

In the past few people took trips in cars.

Today, many people take trips
in cars.

In the past people travelled across oceans in large ships.

Today, people can travel across oceans in aeroplanes.

Who travels?

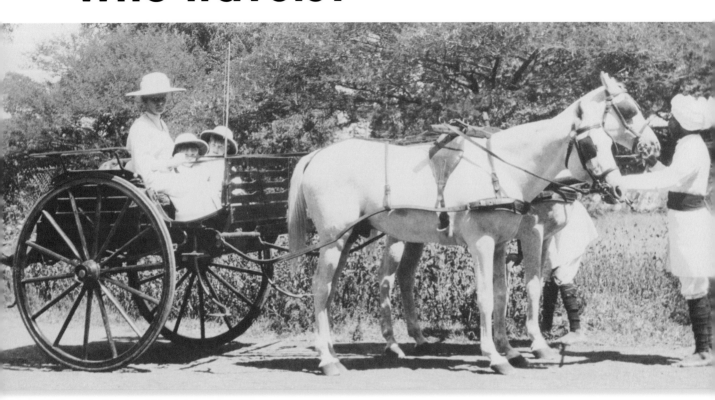

In the past only rich families went on long trips.

Today, many families go on
long trips.

How long did it take?

In the past it could take weeks to
travel to a new place.

Today, people can travel around the world in just hours.

Why travel?

In the past some people travelled far away to start a new life.

Today, people also travel for work and to see new places.

Then and now

In the past people went on trips for fun.
Today, people still go on trips for fun!

Picture glossary

aeroplane large machine that flies through the air

ship large boat that carries many people a long way

Index

Notes for parents and teachers

Before reading

Talk to children about the difference between the past and present. Explain that things that have already happened are in the past. Remind children of a classroom activity that took place a day or two ago, and explain how that activity happened in the past. Then explain that the conversation you are having now is in the present.

After reading

- Explain to children that the way people travel has changed over time. Ask children to think of different modes of transport, such as car, bicycle, aeroplane, or train. Then explain that some of these modes of transport did not exist in the past.

- Tell children that the word *hoilday* means a special trip people take to enjoy themselves. Ask children if they have ever taken a hoilday. If so, ask them to explain where they went, how they got there, and how long the trip took. Then, as a group, brainstorm about how the trip might have been different if it had taken place in the past.

- Ask children if they have ever seen or rode a horse. Explain that in the past, many people used horses for transport. Show children the photo on page 10. Ask if they think travelling by horse would have been fast or slow.